Who Was

Beatrix Potter?

Who Was
Beatrix Potter?

By Sarah Fabiny

Illustrated by Mike Lacey

Grosset & Dunlap
An Imprint of Penguin Random House

For my sisters, Anne and Kathleen, who were very often
the well-behaved Flopsy and Mopsy to my naughty Peter—SF

GROSSET & DUNLAP
Penguin Young Readers Group
An Imprint of Penguin Random House LLC

The publisher does not have any control over and does not assume any responsibility for
author or third-party websites or their content.

Text copyright © 2015 by Sarah Fabiny. Illustrations copyright © 2015
by Penguin Random House LLC. All rights reserved. Published by Grosset & Dunlap,
an imprint of Penguin Random House LLC, 345 Hudson Street, New York,
New York 10014. GROSSET & DUNLAP is a trademark of Penguin Random House LLC.
Printed in the USA.

Library of Congress Cataloging-in-Publication Data is available.

ISBN 978-0-448-48305-4   10 9 8 7 6 5 4 3 2 1

Contents

Who Was
Beatrix Potter?

Early on the morning of April 1, 1897, the
Linnean Society in London, England, gathered to
hear a research paper by Miss Beatrix Potter. The
Linnean Society was a group of men interested
in science. Beatrix's paper was about mushrooms.
Beatrix had also included detailed drawings of
mushrooms. She had drawn many pictures of
mushrooms when she was
a young girl, but she
also loved to draw
pictures of animals.
She dreamed of
becoming a scientist
and continuing her
research on mushrooms.

But her dream could not come true. Women
were not allowed to be members of scientific
societies or participate in meetings. Women were
expected to be wives and mothers. Because Beatrix
could not attend the meeting, her paper was read
by a man. She knew that her research would not be
taken seriously. She was disappointed that her hard
work would not be given the attention it deserved.

But Beatrix was determined that the Linnean
Society's decision would not stop her from doing

something she loved. She was a skilled artist. She could draw almost anything in great detail. She decided to keep drawing the animals she had loved to sketch as a young girl: frogs, lizards, hedgehogs, mice, and rabbits. She would bring them to life and give them stories of their own. She would write about these animals, their friendships, and their adventures.

And that's just what she did. Beginning with *The Tale of Peter Rabbit*, Beatrix Potter went on to publish twenty-nine books during her lifetime. They have sold millions of copies worldwide. And children all over the world still love reading about Beatrix Potter's animal friends.

Chapter 1
A Private World

Helen Beatrix Potter was born on July 28, 1866. She was the first child of Helen and Rupert Potter.

Because her mother was also named Helen, Beatrix was called by her middle name. The Potters lived at Two Bolton Gardens, a big house in a fashionable neighborhood in London. Both of Beatrix's parents came from wealthy families. Although both families had earned their money through hard work, the Potters no longer had to work. They led a very comfortable and carefree life.

Like many parents at the time, Rupert and Helen Potter did not change the way they lived because they had a child. Mr. Potter went to his club and Mrs. Potter visited friends while Beatrix stayed at home with her nanny. One of the rules in the Potter household was that Beatrix was to be seen and not heard, and maybe not even seen that much.

When Beatrix was five years old, her brother, Bertram, was born. Beatrix was excited to finally have someone to share her life with.

Beatrix and Bertram spent almost all their time in the nursery. It was on the top floor of the Potters' big house. Both children were imaginative and creative. They collected all kinds of creatures that lived in the garden.

Nurse Mackenzie was Beatrix's nanny. She told Beatrix stories from Scotland, where she was from. The stories were often about fairies and witches who lived in magical forests. After Bertram was born, Miss Hammond came to work for the Potters. She taught the children school subjects. She also taught them to draw and paint. Beatrix loved her art lessons with Miss Hammond.

Cox, the butler, helped sneak animals from the garden up to Beatrix and Bertram's bedroom.

Over the years, the third-floor "collection" included frogs, rabbits, lizards, mice, a snake, bats, a duck, snails, and hedgehogs. The animals were kept in cages. But they were allowed out when the children were sketching and drawing them.

Helen Potter was a stern mother. As a girl, she had enjoyed drawing, dancing, and needlework. But once she became a wife and mother, she spent her time keeping a tidy and orderly house.

HELEN POTTER

She made sure Beatrix and Bertram lived by certain rules. They were always in clean, starched clothes, their hair was always combed, and their faces and hands were always scrubbed clean. She didn't want Beatrix and Bertram to have friends because she believed that other children carried germs. Her son and daughter might get sick!

Rupert Potter was more loving. He also liked to sketch, and he was interested in the new art of photography. When he saw that his daughter had a talent for drawing, Rupert Potter encouraged it. He often took her to visit museums and the studios of artists who were his friends. Mr. Potter introduced Beatrix to the artist John Everett Millais.

She visited his studio often and had a chance to
see how an artist worked and lived.

JOHN EVERETT MILLAIS (1829–1896)

JOHN EVERETT MILLAIS WAS PART OF A GROUP OF ARTISTS CALLED THE PRE-RAPHAELITE BROTHERHOOD. FOUNDED IN 1848, THE GROUP WANTED TO CREATE IMAGES THAT LOOKED REAL INSTEAD OF ROMANTIC. THE PRE-RAPHAELITES USED BRIGHT COLORS AND INCLUDED LOTS OF DETAIL IN THEIR WORK.

ONE OF MILLAIS'S MOST FAMOUS PAINTINGS IS CALLED *OPHELIA*. THE PAINTING SHOWS THE CHARACTER OPHELIA FROM SHAKESPEARE'S PLAY *HAMLET*. THE PAINTING WAS NOT WELL LIKED WHEN IT WAS FIRST SHOWN. BUT IT IS NOW ADMIRED FOR ITS BEAUTY—ESPECIALLY THE NATURAL LANDSCAPE SURROUNDING OPHELIA.

When Bertram was old enough, his parents sent him to boarding school. Beatrix was once again on her own in the big house at Two Bolton Gardens. Like most wealthy girls at the time, Beatrix did not go to school. She was taught by governesses. And she spent a lot of time drawing and painting in the nursery bedroom. The world of nature fascinated Beatrix. She studied drawings of animals, insects, and plants in her father's books. Beatrix copied them as closely as she could. She wanted to make her drawings look as real as possible. Beatrix worked hard to get the details just right, whether it was a fuzzy caterpillar, a shiny beetle, or a delicate mushroom.

In the summer, the Potters escaped the heat and hustle and bustle of London. At the time, London was the world's largest city. It was also the capital of the British Empire. There were many beautiful gardens and parks in London,

but the city often smelled very bad. There was pollution in the rivers and litter on the streets. Many buildings were covered with soot from factories and coal-burning stoves in homes.

To get away from this, the Potters rented
a house called Dalguise in Scotland.

Beatrix looked forward to these summer
holidays. She loved spending time in the
countryside. Unlike life in London, Beatrix and
Bertram were given lots of freedom at Dalguise.

Beatrix spent many hours exploring the woods and the fields. She studied birds, rabbits, frogs, and squirrels in their natural homes. She wandered through hillsides of purple heather and yellow snapdragons. Beatrix spent hours sketching and painting everything she saw.

Beatrix and Bertram were sad when their summer holidays came to an end and they had to return to London. But they always took some of the countryside with them—caterpillars, minnows, frogs, and insects. They all found homes on the third floor of Two Bolton Gardens.

When she was fifteen, Beatrix began keeping a diary. With very few friends and Bertram away at school, Beatrix shared her secrets and thoughts with her diary. She wrote very, very small so that the words were almost impossible to read. Beatrix also wrote her diary in a special code—a simple letter-for-letter substitution she had made up. This way no one would be able to read what she had written.

Chapter 2
On Her Own

Beatrix began taking art classes at the South
Kensington Museum (now the Victoria and Albert
Museum), which was not far from the Potters' home.
Beatrix was a dedicated and eager student. She
received grades of "excellent" in all her courses.

VICTORIA AND ALBERT MUSEUM

THE VICTORIA AND ALBERT MUSEUM IN LONDON, ENGLAND, CONTAINS MORE THAN 4.5 MILLION OBJECTS—EVERYTHING FROM FRENCH GOWNS AND JEWELRY TO JAPANESE VASES AND ENGLISH FURNITURE.

THE MUSEUM WAS FOUNDED IN 1852 AND WAS ORIGINALLY CALLED THE MUSEUM OF MANUFACTURES. IN 1857, IT WAS RENAMED THE SOUTH KENSINGTON MUSEUM. IN 1899, IT WAS DECIDED THAT THE MUSEUM SHOULD HAVE A BIGGER AND GRANDER BUILDING. THE NEW MUSEUM WAS TO BE CALLED

THE VICTORIA AND ALBERT MUSEUM, AFTER QUEEN
VICTORIA AND PRINCE ALBERT. QUEEN VICTORIA
HAD LAID THE FOUNDATION STONE FOR THE NEW
BUILDING, AND PRINCE ALBERT HAD BEEN A
SUPPORTER OF THE MUSEUM BEFORE HIS DEATH.

TODAY, THE MUSEUM GETS OVER THREE
MILLION VISITORS A YEAR. IT OWNS THE LARGEST
COLLECTION OF BEATRIX POTTER'S DRAWINGS,
MANUSCRIPTS, LETTERS, AND PHOTOGRAPHS IN
THE WORLD.

When Beatrix was almost seventeen,
Mrs. Potter hired Annie Carter to be Beatrix's
governess and German teacher. Annie was just
three years older than her student. Beatrix was
angry. Beatrix felt she was old enough to look
after herself. Her mother was being too protective.

Governesses were for children. But Beatrix and Annie got along very well and soon became good friends. It was the first time in her life that Beatrix had a real friend. She and Annie laughed together and shared secrets.

Beatrix was fascinated by Annie's stories of her life. Although Annie was not much older than Beatrix, she had lived on her own. She had traveled as a student and lived in Germany.

These were things Beatrix could only dream about. Beatrix knew her parents would never agree to let her live on her own, travel, or get a job. Beatrix's parents would make all decisions for her until she was married. This was what all rich parents did for their daughters.

After only two years with the Potters, Annie announced she was leaving to get married. Beatrix was sad and surprised. She was going to lose the only close friend she had ever had. Annie's decision made Beatrix realize how little she really knew about the outside world. Would she ever leave her parents' house? Would she ever become a wife and mother? Would she ever be able to make her own decisions?

Annie Carter married Edwin Moore in 1886. Soon after the wedding, the couple settled in Wandsworth, in southwest London. Annie made Beatrix promise that she would visit. Beatrix knew her parents would not like the idea of her traveling

on her own across the city. But Beatrix was
determined not to lose her dear friend.

BENJAMIN BOUNCER

Not long after Annie left the Potter house, Beatrix bought her first pet rabbit. She named him Benjamin Bouncer. She sneaked him up to the third-floor nursery in a paper bag. Beatrix painted "Bounce" from every angle. In some of the paintings, she even drew little jackets and pants for him to wear!

With Annie gone and Bertram at school, Beatrix had to find things to fill her time. She did the things that she liked best—drawing and painting. She also started thinking more about what she would do with her life. Beatrix put her thoughts in her diary. She did not want to live with her parents forever. She did not want to have to look after them in their old age. But she couldn't go out and get a job. Her parents would never agree to it.

What would become of her?

Chapter 3
Struggles and a Story

In 1885, Beatrix became sick with rheumatic fever. It is a serious illness that can develop after an infection such as strep throat. While Beatrix was ill, most of her hair fell out. She was only nineteen years old. Her hair didn't all grow back, and she had a bald patch for the rest of her life.

The very next year, Beatrix got rheumatic fever again. It made her very sick, and it caused great pain in her arms and legs. It also weakened her heart. Beatrix had to spend a lot of time in bed. For almost eight months, Beatrix didn't write in her journal. But she did paint and draw while she was lying in bed recovering.

As always, Beatrix used the animals that shared her bedroom as her models. Bertram had left two bats at home during one of his visits.

Beatrix let one go, and she spent hours drawing the other. She measured the bones in its wings and legs so that her drawing would be accurate.

Beatrix also used Bertram's microscope to look at beetles, spiders, and butterflies. She wanted her drawings to appear as realistic as possible.

Once Beatrix was better, she convinced her parents to let her visit Annie and Edwin Moore. It was a short journey by carriage, but for Beatrix it was a real adventure.

Beatrix visited the Moores as often as she could. She loved how their house was filled with laughter and delicious smells. And the Moore children, Noel and Eric, were always excited to see Beatrix. She brought Benjamin Bouncer or her pet white mice with her on her visits.

The Moores' home was so different from Beatrix's. There were always hugs and kisses for hellos and good-byes. And everyone ate and played together.

Beatrix was treated like one of the family by Annie and Edwin, their children, and their friends. It made Beatrix worry even more about her future. Would she ever have a home and a life like Annie's? Once again, Beatrix filled her diary with her thoughts. In her special code, she wrote that she felt like life was passing her by.

When Bertram finished school, he decided to move from London to Scotland. He became an artist and painted pictures of the Scottish landscape.

Beatrix always looked forward to her brother's visits. She missed him very much.

During one visit home, Bertram took a look at his sister's work. He told Beatrix that her drawings and paintings were too good not to share.

Bertram convinced Beatrix to send some of her drawings to several publishers. Most of them sent Beatrix's drawings back with a polite no. But one publisher, Hildesheimer & Faulkner, sent Beatrix a check! They wanted to use some of Beatrix's drawings of rabbits on a Christmas card. They also asked if she would be interested in illustrating a book of poetry. Beatrix could hardly believe it! Perhaps she had found a purpose to life. Maybe she, too, could be an artist.

Beatrix's parents were shocked by what she had done. It was fine for Bertram to be an artist and sell his paintings—he was a man. But the Potters did not want their daughter working to earn money. It was simply not something they could allow. Their harsh words upset Beatrix, and she decided to stop drawing and painting. To get away from her parents and their disapproval,

Beatrix visited the Moores as often as possible.
Their happy home made her forget how unhappy
she was at her own.

In September 1893, Annie Moore told Beatrix that Noel, who was nearly six, was ill. Beatrix wasn't able to visit Noel and the rest of the family, so she wrote him a letter instead.

"My dear Noel," the letter started, "I don't know what to write to you, so I shall tell you a story about four little rabbits whose names were Flopsy, Mopsy, Cotton-tail, and Peter. They lived with their mother in a sandbank . . ." Beatrix's letter also had drawings of the four rabbits, their mother, and Mr. McGregor, a mean farmer. Beatrix did not know it, but she had just created what would become the most famous rabbit in the world.

Chapter 4
More Stories to Tell

Beatrix didn't want Noel's younger brother
to feel left out because Noel had received a letter
from her. So the very next day, she sent Eric a
letter about a frog named Mr. Jeremy Fisher.
Annie told Beatrix that the boys were delighted by
her funny stories and drawings in her letters. Over
the years, Annie and Edwin had eight children.

Beatrix wrote more letters to them that told the tales of Squirrel Nutkin, Little Pig Robinson, and the Tailor of Gloucester. Annie Moore realized how special Beatrix's illustrated letters were. She kept them in a safe place.

During this time, Beatrix was also busy studying and painting mushrooms. She had become very interested in mushrooms during her family's vacations in Scotland. Charles McIntosh, the Potters' former mailman at Dalguise House, sent samples of all kinds of mushrooms to Beatrix in London.

Beatrix created over three hundred paintings
of mushrooms! Not only were the images very
detailed and accurate, they were also very beautiful.

Beatrix believed that mushrooms could be used
as medicine and might provide a cure for
cancer. She did research and wrote a report
about what she had discovered. Beatrix was
ready to present her report to the Linnean
Society, a scientific organization in London.

BURLINGTON HOUSE,
HOME TO THE LINNEAN SOCIETY

But just before she was to speak, Beatrix was told
that women were not allowed to be members of
the Linnean Society. A man would have to read
Beatrix's report for her.

Beatrix was very upset. She probably knew
more about mushrooms than anyone in England.
But because Beatrix was a woman and not a
professional scientist, her work was not taken
seriously.

Beatrix gave up her work on mushrooms and went back to drawing and painting animals. She started to think that perhaps she could try to turn her letter to Noel into a book. If the Moore children liked her stories and pictures, perhaps other children would enjoy them, as well.

Beatrix asked Annie if she could borrow the letter about Peter Rabbit. She copied the story and the black-and-white ink drawings of Peter and his siblings into a small sketchbook. Beatrix included one painting in color at the front of the book.

THE TALE OF PETER RABBIT

BEATRIX POTTER'S CLASSIC BOOK TELLS THE STORY OF MRS. RABBIT AND HER FOUR CHILDREN: FLOPSY, MOPSY, COTTON-TAIL, AND PETER. MRS. RABBIT INSTRUCTS HER CHILDREN NOT TO GO INTO MR. MCGREGOR'S GARDEN BECAUSE THEIR FATHER HAD AN ACCIDENT THERE. HE WAS MADE INTO A RABBIT PIE BY MRS. MCGREGOR! FLOPSY, MOPSY, AND COTTON-TAIL LISTEN TO THEIR MOTHER AND HEAD DOWN THE LANE TO PICK BLACKBERRIES. BUT NAUGHTY PETER DISOBEYS HIS MOTHER AND HEADS INTO THE GARDEN TO EAT VEGETABLES. PETER IS SPOTTED BY MR. MCGREGOR. HE LOSES HIS JACKET AND SHOES WHILE TRYING TO ESCAPE. PETER FINALLY MAKES IT BACK HOME, WHERE HIS ANGRY MOTHER SENDS HIM DIRECTLY TO BED. PETER'S WELL-BEHAVED SISTERS HAVE A DELICIOUS SUPPER OF MILK AND BERRIES. BUT PETER IS ONLY ALLOWED A CUP OF CHAMOMILE TEA.

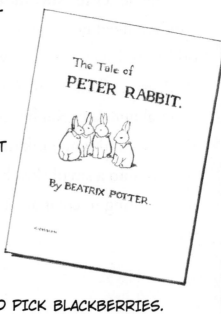

The Tale of
PETER RABBIT.

By BEATRIX POTTER.

SINCE IT WAS FIRST PUBLISHED IN 1902,
THE TALE OF PETER RABBIT HAS BEEN TRANSLATED
INTO OVER THIRTY LANGUAGES AND HAS SOLD
MORE THAN 150 MILLION COPIES WORLDWIDE.

Beatrix then asked her friend Canon Rawnsley to help her send the book to publishers. She and Canon sent the book out six times—and Beatrix got back six rejection letters. A rejection letter meant the publisher didn't want it.

But Beatrix did not let those letters stop her. She decided to use some of the money she had earned from the greeting card to publish the book herself. In December 1901, Beatrix paid to have 250 copies of *The Tale of Peter Rabbit* printed. Beatrix gave copies of the small book to her friends. She also asked a bookstore to take a few copies to sell. The bookstore sold the books very quickly, and they asked Beatrix for more!

She had two hundred additional copies of the book printed. Beatrix had been right after all—people loved the mischievous Peter Rabbit as much as she did. And what a surprise! Even Rupert and Helen Potter seemed to be proud of their daughter's little book.

Canon Rawnsley still wanted a publishing house to print *The Tale of Peter Rabbit.* So he rewrote the story in rhyme and kept Beatrix's drawings. Canon sent that version of the book to a publisher called Frederick Warne & Co. They wrote back saying that they did not like the rhyming story, but they liked the drawings. They also suggested that the drawings would be much better if they were in color.

Beatrix was excited that someone wanted to publish her story of Peter Rabbit! She was happy to go back to her original words, but she didn't want to change her black-and-white ink drawings to color illustrations. She was worried that it would cost too much to print the book in color. She wanted the book to be affordable. And there was "also the rather uninteresting color of a good many of the subjects which are most of them rabbit-brown and green."

Norman Warne was the youngest of three brothers who looked after the publishing company. It had been started by their father, Frederick Warne. Norman's older brothers, Harold and Fruing, told him to convince Beatrix to change her mind. It worked!

NORMAN WARNE

After talking with Norman, Beatrix agreed to re-create all the drawings in *The Tale of Peter Rabbit* in color. Norman told Beatrix that he would make sure the book looked exactly the way she wanted it.

Beatrix expected her book about her beloved rabbit to be perfect. She wanted the colors of the printed illustrations to look like her drawings.

She wanted a certain texture and color for the paper. The style and size of the type had to be just right for readers. She even went to the printing press to watch the book be printed! *The Tale of Peter Rabbit* was published in October 1902. Frederick Warne & Co. printed eight thousand copies. The book was very popular and sold out quickly.

The Tale of Peter Rabbit had to be reprinted several times. By the end of the year, over twenty-eight thousand copies had been printed. By the end of 1903, more than fifty thousand copies of *The Tale of Peter Rabbit* had been sold! Beatrix finally had created something of her own. She would be able to earn her own money as a respected author and illustrator. Her story, and the story of her naughty rabbit, was only beginning.

Chapter 5
Success and Sadness

The Tale of Peter Rabbit was a huge success. And the success of the book gave Beatrix confidence. She had found something she loved and was good at. Beatrix wanted to write more stories for children.

But Beatrix wasn't sure that her publisher would be interested in new stories. She decided to publish *The Tailor of Gloucester* herself and had five hundred copies printed. It was the story of a tailor who  needs to make a vest for the mayor. When he doesn't finish his sewing on time, mice secretly finish it for him. Of all the stories she wrote, *The Tailor of Gloucester* was Beatrix's favorite. And she was wrong about Frederick Warne not wanting more stories. After seeing Beatrix's private edition of the story, the publisher asked her to shorten it a bit and then brought it out in October 1903.

Norman Warne asked Beatrix if she had any other stories. Little did he know how full of stories she was! Beatrix knew that Annie Moore had kept the illustrated letters for her children. Beatrix asked Annie if she could borrow them.

She would turn these letters into books, too. *The Tale of Squirrel Nutkin* was also published in 1903. It was as popular as *The Tale of Peter Rabbit*. Letters from children around the country poured in. They loved Beatrix's characters. "May your bunnies and squirrels live forever!" one child wrote.

Beatrix had never been happier. She loved creating stories. And now they were finding their way out into the world. She also enjoyed working with Norman Warne. Beatrix trusted Norman's advice. And Norman was impressed by Beatrix's talent and knowledge. The two became very close friends. Beatrix also loved spending time with the Warne family. Their home was very different than the Potters'. Norman had lots of cousins, nephews, and nieces, and they all welcomed Beatrix into the family—especially Norman's sister Amelia, whom they called Millie. She was like the sister that Beatrix never had.

THE ART OF BEATRIX POTTER

THE ANIMAL CHARACTERS IN BEATRIX POTTER'S BOOKS OFTEN WEAR CLOTHES AND DO THINGS THAT HUMAN BEINGS DO. IT IS EASY TO THINK OF THEM AS FUNNY, FURRY PEOPLE. BUT THE ANIMALS IN THE PAINTINGS ARE DRAWN IN VERY ACCURATE DETAIL.

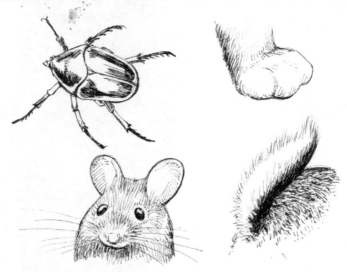

BEATRIX SPENT YEARS STUDYING NATURE AND WORKING HARD TO DEVELOP HER ARTISTIC TALENTS. FROM THE WHISKERS ON MICE TO THE FUR OF A RABBIT TO THE SKIN OF A LIZARD, BEATRIX FELT IT WAS IMPORTANT TO SHOW ANIMALS EXACTLY AS THEY APPEAR IN NATURE. THEIR CHARM AND REALISTIC APPEARANCE ARE WHAT STILL APPEAL TO CHILDREN TODAY.

In 1904, Frederick Warne & Co. published Beatrix's *The Tale of Benjamin Bunny* and *The Tale of Two Bad Mice. The Tale of Benjamin Bunny* continues the story of Peter Rabbit. Peter and his cousin Benjamin return to Mr. McGregor's garden to look for Peter's lost coat and shoes. And Beatrix used her two pet mice, Hunca Munca and Tom Thumb, as the models for the two naughty mice in the story.

Beatrix was happier than she ever had been. Her friendship with Norman had grown into something deeper. They had fallen in love. In July 1905, Norman Warne proposed to her. Beatrix was almost forty years old at the time. She knew

her parents would not approve. They believed
Beatrix should marry someone from a higher social
class. Norman and his family were *tradespeople*—
people who had to work for a living. But Beatrix
and Norman loved each other, and Beatrix felt she
had the right to make this decision herself.

Beatrix's parents asked their daughter not to tell anyone of the engagement. They wanted Beatrix to join them on their vacation to Wales so that Beatrix could think about her decision. They were hoping Beatrix would change her mind after spending time away from Norman. Beatrix was not happy about the trip, but she agreed. She wore her engagement ring when she left for Wales.

Beatrix was working on two more books at the time: *The Tale of Mrs. Tiggy-Winkle* and *The Tale of the Pie and the Patty-Pan*. The character of Mrs. Tiggy-Winkle was a hedgehog. She was based on the washerwoman at Dalguise House in Scotland. *The Tale of the Pie and the Patty-Pan* is the story of a tea party that Ribby the cat gives for Duchess the dog.

Beatrix had been on vacation with her parents for just a few weeks when she received a letter from Millie Warne. The letter said that Norman was very ill. Beatrix wanted to return to London to be with him. But sadly, Norman died before she could make the trip. Beatrix was heartbroken. She had lost the only man she had ever loved.

Because Beatrix wasn't going to get married, she would be expected to remain with her parents in their house. Without a husband, she would spend the rest of her life looking after her parents in their old age.

But Beatrix had other plans.

Chapter 6
A Home of Her Own

After Norman's death, Beatrix wasn't sure how she would still write and draw. Norman had believed in her and her work. They had been a great team, bringing Beatrix's stories to life. Millie Warne was a comfort to Beatrix during this time. She knew that her brother Norman would want Beatrix to keep working. The children of the world needed to have more stories from the Peter Rabbit lady.

Beatrix had been looking forward to moving away from Two Bolton Gardens. Now she would not be starting a new life with Norman. However, Beatrix decided to start a new life on her own. She had earned a lot of money from the sales of her books.

In October 1905, Beatrix bought Hill Top Farm. It was in the village of Near Sawrey in the Lake District in northwest England. England's highest mountain is in this rural area, as well as its longest and deepest lakes.

It is also home to a wide range of wildlife—from red squirrels to golden eagles to wild ponies. It was a bold move for a woman of her time to buy a farm in the Lake District on her own. It was an even bolder move for Beatrix to buy property so far away from her parents.

"It is my heaven," Beatrix told Millie Warne.
Beatrix's parents still expected her to spend time
with them in London, but she escaped to the Lake
District often. It was a different world. The farm
was quiet, and the surrounding fields and woods
were full of the animals that Beatrix loved.

Hill Top Farm was a thirty-four-acre working farm. Beatrix wanted to have a large garden and keep cows, sheep, pigs, and chickens. But the farm needed a lot of work. Beatrix decided that she would make the repairs herself. John Cannon was the farmhand who still lived there with his family.

Beatrix planned to build a new addition onto the farmhouse for the Cannon family. She would live in the original part of the farmhouse.

Just as she always wanted her paintings to be perfect in every detail, Beatrix also wanted her farm to be perfect. She wanted the farmhouse to be repaired properly. And she made sure that the addition was just right for John's family. Beatrix worked to restore the garden, the orchard, and the other buildings on the property. Beatrix's books had earned her money. But now her farm would earn money, as well.

Spending time at Hill Top Farm inspired

Beatrix to start writing and painting again. In the summer of 1906, Beatrix published a book she and Norman had begun working on together, *The Tale of Mr. Jeremy Fisher.* The book was based on one of the letters she had written to the Moore children. Beatrix was pleased that it was now going to be published.

Beatrix was happy to be busy. After *Jeremy Fisher*, *The Story of Miss Moppet*, *The Story of a Fierce Bad Rabbit*, *The Tale of Tom Kitten*, and *The Tale of Jemima Puddle-Duck* soon followed. The rats that had once overrun Hill Top Farm became the inspiration for *The Roly-Poly Pudding*, which was published in 1908.

Beatrix enjoyed her time in Near Sawrey. The residents of the small Lake District village welcomed her. Although she was a famous author, she fit right in with the people of the village. Mr. Cannon had taught Beatrix how to raise animals. Beatrix decided to start breeding sheep. She brought a rare breed of Herdwick sheep to Hill Top Farm. She began showing the sheep at fairs around the Lake District. Beatrix was soon winning prizes for her special sheep!

Just as planned, she started earning money from the farm, as well. Beatrix had found something else that she enjoyed and was good at. Rupert and Helen Potter were pleased that their daughter had invested her money in Hill Top Farm. They thought it was a wise move for Beatrix to buy land with the money she had earned. But they did not want her to actually work on the farm. They thought her interest in farming was just a silly hobby. Beatrix's parents still expected her to spend as much as time as possible with them in London. As an unmarrried daughter, it was her duty. But by now, Beatrix was following her own dreams.

Chapter 7
A New Chapter

Beatrix was putting the sadness of Norman's death behind her. She was writing and painting again. She published ten books in the first nine years after moving to Hill Top Farm. And the farm and the surrounding landscapes found their way into Beatrix's books. She even managed to include some of Near Sawrey's residents in her stories. Disguised as animals, of course!

Not only was Beatrix creating more books, her books were also finding more readers. They were being sold in more bookstores. They were also on the shelves of many libraries. And readers in other countries were also reading about Peter, Benjamin, Jeremy, and Jemima. Beatrix's books were translated into French, German, and Spanish.

The books were also sold in the United States. Beatrix was happy that children all over the world were enjoying her stories.

On the farm, Beatrix wanted more space for her Herdwick sheep, dairy cows, and beef cattle. In the summer of 1909, Beatrix learned that another farm was for sale. It was right next to Hill Top Farm. This was the perfect solution.

WILLIAM HEELIS

Beatrix contacted William Heelis, a local lawyer, to help her buy the farm. William was a tall, quiet man who had lived his whole life in the Lake District. He loved the area as much as Beatrix. He also liked farming and raising animals.

The new farm needed work. William helped Beatrix make improvements and put in a water pipe for the property. They began spending more and more time together.

The new farm took much of Beatrix's time and energy. But she continued to write. In October 1909, she published *The Tale of the Flopsy Bunnies*.

It continued the story of Peter Rabbit and his cousin Benjamin Bunny. *The Tale of Mrs. Tittlemouse* was published in 1910, *The Tale of Timmy Tiptoes* followed in 1911, and *The Tale of Mr. Tod* in 1912.

Writing and farming were what made Beatrix happy. Unfortunately, all the hard work was making her ill. She came down with a high fever and felt dizzy. She had to stay in bed. Her parents were worried about her. They insisted she come to London to rest and get better. Beatrix did not want to leave Near Sawrey, but she agreed. She was too weak to argue with them.

It was difficult for Beatrix to be away from her home in the Lake District. She knew that John Cannon would look after the animals, the orchards, and the garden. But she missed the fresh air, the open spaces, and the peace and quiet. And she missed William. By this time, Beatrix and William had fallen in love. So Beatrix waited for the mail to be delivered every day. She looked forward to receiving letters from William and news from the countryside.

Toward the end of 1912, Beatrix was finally well enough to return home. Soon after, William Heelis proposed to Beatrix. She happily accepted his proposal.

On October 15, 1913, Beatrix and William were married. Their wedding photo tells a lot about the couple. They are both dressed very simply. They are looking straight at the camera.

Their expressions are quiet and strong. It is clear that they care for each other very much and are determined to make a life together. Beatrix was forty-seven years old and had waited a long time for this happy moment.

In the same month that Beatrix and William were married, Frederick Warne & Co. published *The Tale of Pigling Bland.* It is the only book that Beatrix wrote that included a bit of a love story. It tells the story of Pigling Bland and his adventures in the world. His life changes when he meets Pig-wig, "the perfectly lovely little black Berkshire pig."

Chapter 8
A Changing World

Beatrix settled into married life. And she and William enjoyed looking after the farm and all their animals. Beatrix was happy to let go of being Beatrix Potter the author, and enjoyed being Mrs. William Heelis, wife and farmer.

But being a farmer was a lot of work. Beatrix had less time for writing and painting. She hardly ever traveled to London anymore.

But in May 1914, Beatrix had to make the trip for a very sad reason. Her father had died. Beatrix did not always get along with her mother, but she had happy memories of time spent with her father. He had taken her to artists' studios, museums, and art galleries. He had encouraged her to paint and draw.

Beatrix did not want her mother to be on her own in London. She and William invited Helen Potter to move to Castle Cottage Farm with them.

Once her mother arrived, Beatrix had even
less time to write. Beatrix was getting older. Her
eyesight wasn't as good as it used to be, and her
hands were getting stiff. It was difficult for her to
draw and paint as well as she had in the past.

In August 1914, England declared war on
Germany. This was the start of World War I.

Many of the men who lived in the Lake District
worked on farms, including Beatrix and William's
farms. Now these men left England to fight the
war in Europe. Without help, life on the farm
became even more demanding for Beatrix.

Beatrix was still earning money from the sales of her books. But she wasn't earning very much. Her books were as popular as ever, and Frederick Warne & Co. was selling lots of copies. But her payments were less and less. Ever since Norman's death, Beatrix had been working with Harold Warne, Norman's oldest brother. Beatrix wrote to Harold asking why her payments were so low. When Beatrix did not hear back from Harold, she wrote directly to Fruing, the middle Warne brother.

HAROLD AND FRUING WARNE

Fruing discovered Beatrix wasn't being paid all the money that she was owed! Frederick Warne & Co. was in trouble. And it turned out that Harold Warne had been stealing money from his own family's company. In April 1917, Harold went to prison for forgery.

Beatrix knew that the best thing for her to do was to write some new books. This would help her publisher get out of debt. And it would earn Beatrix the money she needed to keep the farms going.

Frederick Warne & Co. published *Appley Dapply's Nursery Rhymes* in 1917. It was a selection of Beatrix's favorite nursery rhymes. And in December 1918, one month after World War I ended, *The Tale of Johnny Town-Mouse* was published.

APPLEY DAPPLY'S
NURSERY RHYMES

BY BEATRIX POTTER

F. WARNE & CO.

Both books were huge successes. One reviewer said, "Miss Potter need not worry about rivals. She has none."

Beatrix and William were now able to focus on farm life. Beatrix was fifty-two years old. Although the characters in her books had given her much joy, she now wanted to concentrate on her life in the country. Because her latest books had been so popular, Fruing Warne asked her to write more. But Beatrix told him, "I am utterly tired of doing them, and my eyes are wearing out."

Beatrix continued to buy farms that were for sale in the area. She looked after the land and often turned the farmhouses into museums that paid tribute to the way of life in the Lake District. She wanted to keep the fields and woods in their natural state. She had footpaths created on her property so that tourists and hikers could visit without disturbing the wildlife or trampling the flowers and plants.

In 1921, a woman named Anne Carroll Moore was visiting the Lake District. She was from New York City, where she was head of Children's Services for the New York

ANNE CARROLL MOORE

Public Library. She wrote Beatrix and asked if she could visit. Beatrix did not usually like to have visitors in her home. But she agreed to speak with Anne Carroll Moore.

Anne Moore told Beatrix that her writing was greatly admired in the United States. Beatrix was pleased by this. In England, Beatrix felt that people sometimes loved her illustrations more than her writing. It made her happy to hear that Americans thought her words were as beautiful as the pictures she painted. With Anne Moore's words in her head, Beatrix decided to work on a new project. *Cecily Parsley's Nursery Rhymes* came out for Christmas 1922.

Chapter 9
A Special Legacy

Beatrix loved her life in the Lake District. She enjoyed breeding her prizewinning sheep, looking after her property, and spending time with her husband's family. Her life as a children's book author seemed further and further away.

In 1924, the Potter family home at Two Bolton Gardens, South Kensington, London, was sold. Although Beatrix's mother was still alive

and lived with her and William, Beatrix felt
she could finally close that chapter
of her life.

Beatrix's American publisher had asked her for one more book. Her stories were popular in the United States, and Beatrix appreciated the American readers. She did not want to disappoint them. *The Tale of Little Pig Robinson* was published in 1930,

both in England and America. The book was a success in both countries. Beatrix had published twenty-three best-selling books in fewer than thirty years. What an accomplishment!

When Beatrix's mother died in 1932, Beatrix no longer had to worry about looking after her parents. She didn't have to behave or dress in a way that reflected well on her family. Beatrix started wearing the clothes that *she* wanted to wear. She was often seen walking through her fields with an old sack over her shoulders. She wore men's boots and old sweaters.

But Beatrix didn't care what people thought about her. She was happy with her life with William in Near Sawrey.

World War II broke out in 1939. Once again, the events of the world touched the Lake District.

BRITISHERS
ENLIST TO·DAY
44 BROMFIELD STREET

Men were called away to be soldiers. And this time there was much more for Beatrix and William to worry about. They were both older now. It took a lot of time and energy to keep the farms going.

One of Beatrix's greatest joys at this time was having the Girl Guides (the name for the Girl Scouts in England) camp on her property.

Many of the girls were from the city. Spending time on Beatrix's farms was their first experience of open spaces and fresh air. Beatrix remembered how much she enjoyed her family vacations in Scotland as a child. She felt it was important for the Girl Guides to live in the English countryside.

On Beatrix's seventieth birthday, the Girl
Guides surprised her with a special party. They
came to the farm dressed as characters from her
books. Beatrix was deeply touched. Just before

Christmas 1943, Beatrix became sick with
bronchitis, an infection of the lungs. She had
suffered from the illness her whole life. But now
she was older, and her heart was much weaker.
This time she did not recover.

Beatrix Potter died on December 22, 1943. William was at her side when she passed away at Castle Cottage Farm. Although she was famous all over the world, she had led a simple and modest life. When she died, Beatrix Potter left the farmland she had bought in the Lake District—

more than four thousand acres—to the National
Trust. It meant that the land would remain as it
was, wild and natural.

THE NATIONAL TRUST

THE NATIONAL TRUST IS A CHARITABLE ORGANIZATION DEDICATED TO PRESERVING IMPORTANT AREAS AND PLACES IN ENGLAND, WALES, AND NORTHERN IRELAND. IT MAINTAINS CASTLES, MANOR

HOUSES, GARDENS, FORESTS, BEACHES, AND FARMS. THE ORGANIZATION WAS FOUNDED IN 1895 BY OCTAVIA HILL, SIR ROBERT HUNTER, AND CANON RAWNSLEY. THEY WANTED TO MAKE SURE THAT THERE WERE OPEN, NATURAL SPACES THAT WOULD NOT BE BUILT ON—SPACES THAT EVERYONE WOULD BE ABLE TO VISIT AND ENJOY. TODAY, THE NATIONAL TRUST LOOKS AFTER MORE THAN THREE HUNDRED HISTORIC BUILDINGS AND MORE THAN SIX HUNDRED THOUSAND ACRES OF LAND. MORE THAN EIGHTEEN MILLION PEOPLE VISIT NATIONAL TRUST SITES EVERY YEAR.

Beatrix wanted the land to be preserved so that everyone could enjoy it. She also gave children around the world her twenty-three "tales" and other books. "If I have done anything," Beatrix wrote, "even a little, to help children on the road to enjoy and appreciate honest, simple pleasures, I have done a bit of good."

TIMELINE OF
BEATRIX POTTER'S LIFE

1866 — Born July 28 in London, England

1872 — Brother Bertram born March 14

1880 — Awarded art student's certificate for model drawing and freehand from the South Kensington Museum

1883 — Bertram sent to boarding school
Annie Carter becomes Beatrix's governess

1890 — Sells drawings to Hildesheimer & Faulkner that are used for greeting cards

1897 — Scientific paper on mushrooms presented to the Linnean Society of London

1901 — Privately prints 250 copies of *The Tale of Peter Rabbit*

1902 — Frederick Warne & Co. publishes *The Tale of Peter Rabbit* and prints eight thousand copies

1905 — Buys Hill Top Farm

1909 — Buys Castle Cottage Farm

1913 — Marries William Heelis

1921 — Anne Carroll Moore, superintendent of Children's Services, New York Public Library, visits Beatrix

1923 — Buys Troutbeck Park Farm

1930 — Buys the five-thousand-acre Monk Coniston Estate
Publishes last *Tale* book, *The Tale of Little Pig Robinson*

1943 — Dies on December 22, at the age of seventy-seven

1958 — The secret code used in Beatrix's journal is cracked

TIMELINE OF THE WORLD

Lewis Carroll's *Alice's Adventures in Wonderland* is published	1865
The Suez Canal opens	1869
Alexander Graham Bell invents the telephone	1876
New Zealand is the first country to give women the right to vote	1893
Queen Victoria dies	1901
Rudyard Kipling's *Just So Stories* is published	1902
Henry Ford introduces the Model T car	1908
The *Titanic* sinks	1912
World War I begins in Europe	1914
Albert Einstein proposes the theory of general relativity	1915
World War I ends	1918
A.A. Milne publishes *Winnie-the-Pooh*	1926
Discovery of penicillin by Alexander Fleming	1928
Wall Street crash sparks the Great Depression	1929
Franklin D. Roosevelt is elected president of the United States	1932
World War II begins in Europe	1939
H.A. and Margret Rey's *Curious George* is published	1941

BIBLIOGRAPHY

Potter, Beatrix. **Beatrix Potter: A Journal**. New York: Warne, 2006.

Potter, Beatrix. **Beatrix Potter's Letters**. Edited by Judy Taylor. London: Warne, 1989.

* Buchan, Elizabeth. **Beatrix Potter: The Story of the Creator of Peter Rabbit**. New York: Warne, 1998.

* Collins, David R. **The Country Artist: A Story about Beatrix Potter**. Minneapolis: Carolrhoda Books, 1989.

* Guillain, Charlotte. **Beatrix Potter**. Chicago: Heinemann Library, 2012.

Lear, Linda. **Beatrix Potter: A Life in Nature**. New York: Allen Lane, 2008.

* Books for young readers

* Wallner, Alexandra. **Beatrix Potter**. New York: Holiday House, 1995.

* Winter, Jeanette. **Beatrix**. New York: Farrar, Straus and Giroux, 2003.

WEBSITES

biographyonline.net/writers/beatrix-potter.html

peterrabbit.com

beatrixpottersociety.org.uk

THE 23 "TALE" BOOKS BY BEATRIX POTTER

1902   *The Tale of Peter Rabbit*

1903   *The Tale of Squirrel Nutkin*
       The Tailor of Gloucester

1904   *The Tale of Benjamin Bunny*
       The Tale of Two Bad Mice

1905   *The Tale of Mrs. Tiggy-Winkle*
       The Tale of The Pie and The Patty-Pan

1906   *The Tale of Mr. Jeremy Fisher*
       The Story of a Fierce Bad Rabbit
       The Story of Miss Moppet

1907   *The Tale of Tom Kitten*

1908   *The Tale of Jemima Puddle-Duck*
       The Roly-Poly Pudding
       (later renamed *The Tale of Samuel Whiskers*)

1909   *The Tale of the Flopsy Bunnies*
       The Tale of Ginger and Pickles

1910   *The Tale of Mrs. Tittlemouse*

1911   *The Tale of Timmy Tiptoes*

1912   *The Tale of Mr. Tod*

1913   *The Tale of Pigling Bland*

1917   *Appley Dapply's Nursery Rhymes*

1918   *The Tale of Johnny Town-Mouse*

1922   *Cecily Parsley's Nursery Rhymes*

1930   *The Tale of Little Pig Robinson*